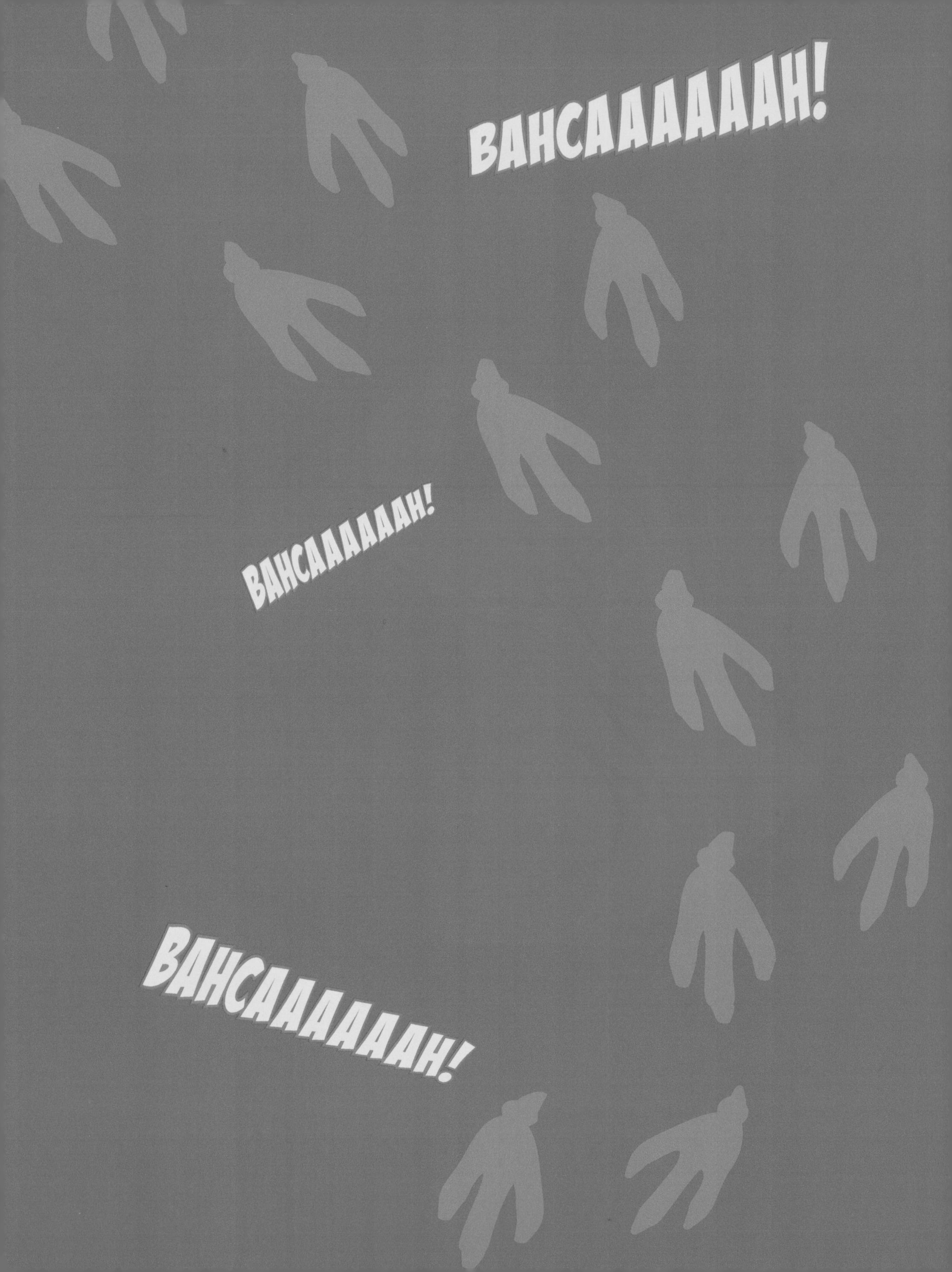
BAHCAAAAAAH!
BAHCAAAAAAH!
BAHCAAAAAAH!

CHICKEN BOY

The Amazing Adventures of a Super Hero With Autism

Written by Gregory G. Allen
Illustrated by Dennis Culver

BAHCAAAAAAH!

BAHCAAAAAAH!

Chicken Boy: The Amazing Adventures of a Super Hero with Autism
Copyright © 2012 by Gregory G. Allen. All rights reserved.
Originally published by MeeGenius "eBooks for Kids"
Print Version published by ASD Publishing
ISBN: 978-0-9853441-0-8
Library of Congress Control Number: 2012904616
Print book design by Janine A. Wentz, W Design, LLC.
Manufactured in the United States of America

www.asdpublishing.com

Inspired by Gabe
Created with Natalie

BAHCAAAA AAH !

I call him Chicken Boy.

Doctors say I have autism,
which is a fancy word…

For me living inside my own brain.

When I eat chicken fingers, ketchup, and French fries, Chicken Boy comes out.

People sometimes look at me
when I make my superhero sound.

That's because they can't see
my superhero powers.

But even superheroes have a weak spot. Chicken Boy can't handle crying babies.

Sometimes I run away
from the loud noise
out into the rain.

No one can understand why
Chicken Boy finds it
peaceful and fun.

For me that's
MY superhero energy
falling from the sky.

It's also sometimes hard for me to talk and play with others.

But that doesn't mean that I don't want to.

It just might take
a little more effort
to get me to do it.

If you ever see someone like me…

Don't be scared.

Just take time to get to know me.

Maybe you can be a superhero with me.

CPSIA information can be obtained
at www.ICGtesting.com
Printed in the USA
BVHW020908100422
633712BV00001B/5